# Discover your Spiritual Gifts

## A PERSONAL INVENTORY METHOD

# Kenneth Cain Kinghorn

Discovering Your Spiritual Gifts: A Personal Inventory and Method
Copyright © 1981 by Kenneth Cain Kinghorn

Requests for information should be addressed to:
Zondervan Publishing House
Grand Rapids, Michigan 49530


**Library of Congress Cataloging in Publication Data**

Kinghorn, Kenneth C.
    Discovering your spiritual gifts.

    Reprint. Originally published: Wilmore, Ky.:
F. Asbury, c1981.
    Bibliography: p.
    1. Gifts, Spiritual.  I. Title.
BT767.3.K55    1984        234'.13        84-5665
ISBN 0-310-75661-X


This book was originally published by the Francis Asbury Publishing Company, Inc., under the title *Discovering Your Spiritual Gifts: A Personal Method.* All publication rights have been assigned to Zondervan Publishing House.

Scripture quotations in this publication are from the Revised Standard Version of the Bible, copyrighted 1946, 1952 © 1971, 1973 by the Division of Christian Education of the National Council of the Churches of Christ in the United States of America.

*Printed in the United States of America*

95 96 97 98 99 00 01 02 03/DP/ 28 27 26 25 24 23 22 21

# Table of Contents

# Introduction

This book has been written to help *you* discover *your* spiritual gifts. It identifies and defines each of the spiritual gifts listed in the New Testament. The book also contains an "inventory" of two hundred statements to which you can respond on the enclosed scoring sheet. This inventory is designed to assist you in identifying the specific gifts that God has given to you. At the end of the book I've included a selected list of the best books available on the subject of spiritual gifts.

In response to many requests for practical help in these matters, I've prepared *DISCOVERING YOUR SPIRITUAL GIFTS: A PERSONAL METHOD* as a practical supplement to my book, *GIFTS OF THE SPIRIT* (Abingdon Press). While one can use this present manual by itself, one will be helped a great deal by the more detailed study of spiritual gifts that is found in *GIFTS OF THE SPIRIT*.

The inventory presented in *DISCOVERING YOUR SPIRITUAL GIFTS: A PERSONAL METHOD* has been used effectively by a number of Christians throughout the United States, and I sincerely believe that it will help you to understand which spiritual gifts God has given you.

Best wishes to you as you adventure into this exciting dimension of the Christian life — my prayers remain with you in this experience. Discovering your spiritual gifts can become a turning point for you, as the process sets you free to minister with confidence and joy. May God bless you richly as you embark on this important journey.

Kenneth Cain Kinghorn
Asbury Theological Seminary
Wilmore, Kentucky

# Definition of a Spiritual Gift

The normal New Testament word for a *spiritual gift* is *charisma* (*charismata* in the plural). This term has three uses in the New Testament. (1) In some passages it means God's gift of salvation. An example of this usage is found in the statement, ". . . the free gift *(charisma)* of God is eternal life in Christ Jesus our Lord" (Romans 6:23).

(2) In other cases the term refers to blessing, encouragement, or comfort. For instance, Paul uses the term in this way when referring to God's favor: "You also must help us by prayer, so that many will give thanks on our behalf for the blessing *(charisma)* granted us in answer to many prayers" (II Corinthians 1:11).

(3) Still another important use of the term *charisma* relates to a special ability to minister with effectiveness and power. When used in this context the term *charisma* is best translated "spiritual gift." It is this third use that concerns us in this book. The most significant uses of the terms *charisma* and *charismata* appear in the following references:

> "Having *gifts* that differ according to the grace given to us, let us use them . . ." (Romans 12:6).
>
> "Now there are varieties of *gifts* . . ." (I Corinthians 12:4).
>
> "Earnestly desire the higher *gifts*" (I Corinthians 12:31).
>
> "Do not neglect the *gift* you have . . ." (I Timothy 4:14).
>
> "I remind you to rekindle the *gift* of God that is within you . . ." (II Timothy 1:6).
>
> "As each has received a *gift*, employ it for one another, as good stewards of God's varied grace" (I Peter 4:10).

Spiritual gifts should be distinguished from human talents which can operate without divine assistance. Moreover, spiritual gifts should be distinguished from spiritual fruits: The fruits of the Spirit describe moral virtues (see Galatians 5:22, 23), while spiritual gifts relate to enablings or abilities that equip Christians for service (see Romans 12:6-8; I Peter 4:10).

Precisely stated, a spiritual gift is a divine, supernatural ability given by God to enable a Christian to serve and to minister. More simply put, a spiritual gift is a special tool for ministry.

## Importance of Knowing Your Spiritual Gifts

Sometimes the question is asked, "Can spiritual gifts operate through me if I am not aware of my spiritual gifts?" The answer is, "Of course they can." (Christians in the Middle Ages, for example, did not have an adequate theology of spiritual gifts, yet the gifts of the Spirit certainly flowed through many of their lives.) Most assuredly, one can manifest spiritual gifts without understanding or even being aware of them.

However, there are many good reasons for our knowing and understanding our gifts. We stand in a much more favorable position to become effective disciples when we identify and develop the spiritual gifts God has given us. Specifically, here are some solid reasons for you to become aware of your spiritual gifts:

### The identification of your spiritual gifts

1. *Helps you determine God's will for your vocation.* A knowledge of your gifts will provide a context for making career and ministry decisions regarding what *not* to attempt as well as what to enter into with confidence.

2. *Mobilizes the entire church for mission.* Since a small percentage of the church consists of clergy and more than ninety percent of the church consists of non-clergy, the church obviously must equip and encourage every Christian to minister in his or her respective sphere of influence.

3. *Assists you in setting priorities for study, growth, and ministry.* Since each of us has a limited amount of time to develop our potential, it seems clear that we should develop ourselves in the areas of our special gifts.

4. *Gives each Christian a sense of dignity and self worth.* Every Christian is an important part of the total church. There are no "second class" citizens in the Christian community because each person constitutes a vitally significant member of the body of Christ.

5. *Enables you to receive the gift ministries of others.* When Christians become more knowledgeable of their own spiritual gifts and those of other Christians, they can more easily function harmoniously as the Body of Christ, both giving and receiving ministries.

6. *Fosters unity among fellow Christian believers.* As the members of the church function inter-dependently (not independently), an awareness of spiritual gifts leads them to respect one another as they live together in the common life of the Spirit.

# Spiritual Gifts Identified

Although various biblical writers refer directly or indirectly to spiritual gifts, the Apostle Paul supplies us with the most systematic listing of the Spirit's gifts. The chart* below shows four principle passages where Paul makes specific reference to spiritual gifts.

| Romans 12:6-8 | I Corinthians 12:4-11 | I Corinthians 12:28 | Ephesians 4:11 |
|---|---|---|---|
| Prophecy | Prophecy | Prophecy | Prophecy |
| Teaching | | Teaching | Teaching |
| Serving | | | |
| Exhortation | | | |
| Giving | | | |
| Giving Aid | | | |
| Compassion | | | |
| | Healing | Healing | |
| | Working miracles | Working miracles | |
| | Tongues | Tongues | |
| | Interpretation of tongues | Interpretation of tongues | |
| | Wisdom | | |
| | Knowledge | | |
| | Faith | | |
| | Discernment | | |
| | | Apostleship | Apostleship |
| | | Helps | |
| | | Administration | |
| | | | Evangelism |
| | | | Shepherding |

*This chart is taken from my book, GIFTS OF THE SPIRIT, Abingdon Press, p. 38.

# Spiritual Gifts Described

Here is a brief definition of each of the spiritual gifts listed in the New Testament.

*Administration* is a gift that enables one to provide leadership and guidance in matters of organization and administration. The administrator serves by recognizing and co-ordinating the abilities and gifts of other members of the group, institution, or church.

*Apostleship* is the ability to communicate the Christian message across cultural (and frequently linguistic) barriers and plant a Christian church where there is no knowledge of the gospel. The term in Greek *(apostolos)* and Latin *(missio)* means "a sent one" or "a messenger." The rough modern equivalent is a pioneer missionary.

*Compassion* transcends both natural human sympathy and normal Christian concern, enabling one to sense in others a wide range of emotions and then provide a supportive ministry of caring.

*Discernment* is the ability to read or hear a teaching or to consider a proposed course of action and then determine whether the source behind the teaching or action is divine, human, or satanic.

*Evangelism* is the special ability to lead unconverted persons to a personal knowledge of Jesus Christ. Persons with this gift are able to help others to a life-changing decision which moves them to accept Jesus Christ as Lord and Savior.

*Exhortation* is the ability to call forth the best within others through the ministry of understanding, encouragement, and counsel. This gift equips one to lift up and strengthen others by helping them to move from their problem to a resolution of that problem.

11

*Faith* is the special ability to "see light at the end of the tunnel," even though others are unaware of divine possibilities in a situation. This gift results in one's having extraordinary confidence in God, and it enables that person through prayer to tap God's resources in behalf of others.

*Giving* empowers one in an extraordinary way to understand or discern the material or financial needs of others and then meet those needs generously. The more one uses this gift the more God prospers one so that the person with this gift is enabled to give still more.

*Giving aid* literally means in the Greek "he who provides leadership in giving aid." This gift equips one to see practical needs and co-ordinate the resources and abilities of others so that those needs are met.

*Healing* enables one to function as an instrument of God's healing grace in the lives of others. The gifts of healings (double plural in the Greek text) extend to the healing of the body, the mind, and the emotions.

*Helps* is a gift that leads to practical ministries to others, which relieve them, in turn, to perform still wider ministries.

*Miracles* refer to the superseding of natural law. In the Book of Acts this gift most frequently relates to healing and to exorcism (Eg., Acts 19:11-12).

*Prophecy* is the ability to present God's word with clarity and power. The primary ministry of this gift is not prediction or foretelling; it principally has to do with declaration or forthtelling.

*Teaching* is the ability to understand and communicate the Christian faith so as to make truth clear to others. The end result of this gift is the maturing of Christian believers so that they may be more effective Christian disciples.

*Tongues* enable some Christians to praise God either in another language not yet learned (Acts 2) or in ecstatic utterance which is not an earthly language (I Corinthians 14). In either case one's prayer is addressed to God, not to other people (I Corinthians 14:2).

*Tongues, Interpretation Of:* The interpretation of tongues is required if speaking in tongues is exercised publicly. This gift enables one to interpret to others the intent or meaning of what was uttered to God by the one being interpreted.

*Serving* is a task-oriented ministry that results in the supplying of material and temporal services to others in the Body of Christ, thereby freeing them to perform still other ministries.

*Shepherding* is the ability to give pastoral leadership to an individual or to a community of Christian believers. The primary function of this gift is to feed, guide, and nurture other Christians with sensitivity and sacrificial concern.

*Word of Knowledge* is knowing a fact or the truth about a person or a situation as it is directly revealed by the Holy Spirit.

*Word of Wisdom* relates to a special illumination that enables one in a specific instance to grasp divine insight regarding a fact, situation, or context.

# Discovering Your Spiritual Gifts:
# A Personal Method
## Instructions For Taking the Inventory

This inventory consists of four components:
1. The instructions (this page)
2. Two hundred statements to which you respond (p. 15)
3. The response sheet (centerfold insert)
4. The key (p. 28)

The following exercise provides opportunity for you to respond to two hundred statements about your interest in, and experience of, spiritual gifts. Do not respond on the basis of what you think you *ought* to say. Rather, respond on the basis of your *interest* and your *experience*. Do not let modesty hinder you from answering honestly about your abilities. If a question is not relevant to your experience, then answer it by marking a zero (0) in the proper place. Five (5) is the proper way to record a strongly favorable response.

Rate yourself on the following scale from zero to five:
- 0 The question is not relevant to my experience, or I have no response, or I have a negative response
- 1 Only a slight response
- 2 Little response
- 3 Medium or moderate response
- 4 Greater than average response
- 5 Strong response

When you have completed the response sheet (centerfold insert) add the scores in each *horizontal* line. For example, for line A you will add up the responses to questions 1, 21, 41, 61, 81, 101, 121, 161, and 181. Put your totals in the column marked TOTAL.

Your total score for each horizontal line will suggest your interest or your ability under each category. Of course this evaluation is from your own personal perspective. However, your own assessments constitute an important part of discovering your spiritual gifts.

Fill in the blank spaces under the heading **Gifts,** using the gifts listed in the key on p. 28. The highest scores should indicate your spiritual gifts.

## The Inventory

Remember, as you respond to the following statements on the response sheet (centerfold insert), mark your response on the basis of your interests, experiences, and personal opinion of yourself.

1. I can adapt to different lifestyles in order to establish a Christian witness among foreign people. ○
2. I enjoy showing others how the Bible speaks to their current situation. 3
3. I enjoy leading others to Jesus Christ. 3
4. I like to spend myself in order to help others grow as Christians. 3
5. I tend to see how Christian truths relate to each other as a whole. 3
6. At times I have a strong desire to meet the practical needs of others. 3
7. People often seek me out for counsel and guidance.
8. I receive joy when I can give money for the work of Christ. 3
9. I find fulfillment in working with others to minister to people who need help. 3
10. I am especially drawn to those who are suffering mental 3

or physical anguish.

11. God often leads me to pray for the total healing of others in body, mind, and spirit.
12. God has inspired my prayers so that impossible things have been accomplished.
13. I have spoken in tongues.
14. I have interpreted tongues so as to help others worship God without confusion.
15. Sometimes God gives me an insight as to the proper course of action that others ought to take.
16. I have had times when I became aware of a situation or an event quite apart from any outside communication.
17. Sometimes others have told me that I have great faith.
18. I can easily detect spiritual truth or spiritual error.
19. I enjoy working in the background if I can help others.
20. I work well under pressure and in the midst of activity. I can get to the heart of a matter and take decisive action.
21. I could feel good in taking the gospel to a pagan tribe.
22. I will not compromise the truth even when I am criticized for being stubborn or hard-headed.
23. I find it easy to invite persons to commit themselves to Christ.
24. At times I feel led to go to a straying Christian and help him onto the way.
25. I feel that God has some sort of teaching ministry for me.
26. I enjoy serving others so that they, in turn, may perform their ministries.
27. Others tell me that I am a good counsellor.
28. I believe that God has given me the ability both to make and to share money.
29. If no structured organization exists, I am willing to step forward and assume responsibility for leadership.
30. I think God wants me especially to minister to those in distress.
31. Some have told me they think I have the gift of healing.

32. I believe that God can miraculously alter circumstances if we pray.
33. Praying in tongues has been meaningful to me in my personal prayer life.
34. When others have prayed in tongues I felt that I understood the meaning of their prayer.
35. God enables me to see the proper application of Christian truth to specific circumstances.
36. When in casual conversation with another I have become aware of a deep need within that person which he was careful to hide.
37. I can easily see God's hand at work in the present.
38. I can detect spiritual phoniness before others can.
39. I enjoy assisting others so as to free them for their own ministries.
40. I can recognize talents and gifts in others and also help them to find ways of using their abilities.
41. I would enjoy learning a new language in order to pioneer a new church overseas.
42. I like to tell others about God's judgment for wrongdoing and of his gracious promises to those who turn to him.
43. I like to bear public witness to what Christ has done for me.
44. I tend to be patient with Christians who are making slow progress in the Christian life.
45. I prefer to read profound Christian truth rather than Christian biography.
46. I tend to be one of the first ones to notice the practical needs of others.
47. When encouraging another or giving advice, I am concerned about how that person reacts to my efforts to help.
48. I like to give money anonymously.
49. I feel that I can see the whole picture and help direct

others in making their best contributions to Christian projects.

50. I enjoy rendering practical aid to those who have gotten themselves into trouble.
51. I often pray for others that their pain will be removed.
52. More than once I have prayed and persons have been healed although medical doctors said a cure was impossible.
53. I enjoy praying to God in an ecstatic experience.
54. When I interpret someone's prayer in tongues I always want unbelievers to be present so they can be helped.
55. I seem to be able to apply God's truth to concrete situations.
56. Sometimes I think I can see a situation almost as God sees it.
57. I often see a direct connection between God's promises to his ancient people and his faithfulness today.
58. I often have an insight that a particular book or message is inspired by God.
59. In the church I prefer such ministries as ushering, typing, filing, cleaning, and helping in any way I can.
60. I can inspire others to use their gifts in God's service.
61. I often think that I may be called to take the gospel to a completely unchurched area.
62. I can easily see ways that the Bible relates to current social needs.
63. After sharing the gospel I like to ask persons for a personal decision for Christ.
64. I feel a responsibility to nurture others in Christian discipleship.
65. I find joy in harmonizing and arranging biblical teaching.
66. I don't mind serving others even if I am needed to perform menial tasks.
67. I can identify with the faltering in such a way as to

encourage them to renew their hope and their commitments.

68. I strongly feel that some Christians should give considerably more than their tithe.
69. Sometimes God helps me to organize people and resources in order to meet practical needs.
70. Sometimes I sense when others are hurting inside.
71. I often feel impressed to pray for those who are ill.
72. I find that God is most apt to intervene when the situation looks most hopeless.
73. I first prayed in tongues when I was all alone.
74. When I hear others interpret tongues I sometimes feel that they are more "in the flesh" than "in the Spirit."
75. Other Christians seek my advice when they are uncertain of their direction.
76. At times I have suddenly realized certain options for the church which others did not perceive.
77. I find it easy to trust God even when the faith of others falters.
78. God has often enabled me to encourage others to accept a truly biblical teaching.
79. I like to relieve others of everyday tasks so that they can do important ministries.
80. People often look to me for guidance in organizing and managing.
81. I am excited about the idea of learning a new culture so as to take the gospel to other lands.
82. I feel that God often anoints my public speaking.
83. I would rather evangelize than teach.
84. I want to know and to understand those I am serving.
85. I enjoy preparing and giving an orderly presentation of some portion of scripture.
86. I often recognize ways I can minister to others indirectly, without speaking or teaching.
87. I enjoy helping others work out detailed steps for

becoming better Christian disciples.

88. Sometimes I feel led to give money for specific ministries outside my congregation.
89. Usually I would rather help solve practical problems of everyday life than to teach or to preach.
90. God uses me to console those suffering from depression or discouragement.
91. I sometimes have faith to pray for God's direct intervention in physical illness.
92. Sometimes when I pray God miraculously changes circumstances.
93. I never speak in tongues publicly unless I am strongly impressed to do so and unless someone interprets.
94. When I hear someone speak in tongues, the Holy Spirit gives me the correct interpretation.
95. On some occasions God has helped me bring illumination to other Christians when they have been confused about what course to take.
96. I have had the experience of knowing something even though no one told me.
97. I seldom have difficulty believing God will help persons if they trust Him.
98. I can sometimes detect good in other Christian traditions even when others are slow to recognize it.
99. I would rather keep records for a class than to teach the class.
100. As a leader I can easily delegate authority to others.
101. I am intrigued with the idea of moving into the midst of sub-culture and learning their ways so as to win them for Christ.
102. I find it relatively easy to suffer ridicule for sticking to God's word.
103. I tend to conclude my vocal witness for Christ with an appeal for others to become Christians.
104. I enjoy teaching and guiding a group of Christians.

105. I think it is important to use words accurately and pronounce them properly.
106. I don't mind helping others even if they are not deserving or if they take advantage of me.
107. I like to encourage and counsel with those who are spiritually or emotionally unstable.
108. I view the giving to meet material needs as my special ministry.
109. I receive fulfillment in tapping community resources so as to organize a ministry to those in need.
110. I like to work with those who are neglected by others.
111. I have prayed for persons and they have been healed.
112. Through prayer God has miraculously intervened in my life.
113. When praying in tongues I have wished that I knew what I prayed.
114. Mature Christian pastors have told me that they think I have the gift of interpreting tongues.
115. I can see the several sides of an issue and sense which way God is leading the group.
116. God has given me the direct knowledge of some fact before it was known to others.
117. I can see the hand of God working in times of seeming tragedy.
118. God has used me to warn others of the danger of a certain teaching.
119. I often see small details that need attention before others do.
120. I am willing to make decisions even at the risk of being misunderstood by others.
121. I think that I could be effective in beginning a new church where no church exists.
122. People have often told me that they find my public addresses inspiring.
123. I am troubled when non-Christians are not given an

invitation to accept Christ at the end of a worship service.

124. I enjoy having the responsibility for discipling a group of Christians.
125. I prefer hearing or reading scriptural teaching rather than personal testimonies.
126. I think one of my spiritual gifts is to serve others by helping relieve their material or physical burdens.
127. I like to help others as long as they respond, but when they become disinterested or reject me I move on to another task.
128. God seems to have enabled me to make money, and I love to give liberally to Christian causes.
129. I enjoy working with others to minister in practical ways.
130. I like to visit prisons, homes for the elderly, and other institutions in order to minister, comfort and hope.
131. I often have a strong sense that God wants to heal someone.
132. God has worked spectacular miracles in my life.
133. I sometimes feel I lack the words to praise God as I wish I could.
134. When I hear someone pray in tongues I can usually sense when God is inspiring them and when he isn't.
135. Others tell me that I show maturity in offering advice about spiritual matters.
136. I have had the experience of talking with another person for only a short time and understanding what his real problem was.
137. I can trust God to bring victory to those who seem to have lost faith.
138. I can often sense when a speaker is true to the Bible.
139. I enjoy helping out with little details.
140. I can organize church resources for an effective ministry of social concern.
141. I would enjoy the challenge of a pioneer missionary

assignment.

142. I find it easy to apply biblical promises to human situations.
143. I feel natural leading up to an appeal for others to receive Christ as Savior.
144. I feel that I am responsible to help protect weak Christians from influences that would undermine their faith.
145. I get troubled when I hear or read a radiant testimony when it contains some false teaching or unsound advice.
146. I enjoy working in the background if I can meet practical needs of others.
147. I can challenge others without condemning them.
148. I frequently feel led to give money to certain Christian enterprises.
149. I don't mind calling on others to help me in a worthy Christian project.
150. I feel compassion for the undeserving.
151. I rarely hesitate to pray that the sick will be made well.
152. I believe that if we trusted God more than we presently do we might see miracles today such as those that occurred in the Book of Acts.
153. When I first prayed in tongues no one pressured me to do so.
154. Every time I interpret tongues I want to be sure that I am sensitive to the Holy Spirit and to the mood of the congregation.
155. In a group when I am faced with the request for my opinion about the future direction to be taken, I have been inspired by God to give sound counsel.
156. I have surprised others by telling them something about themselves that they have not revealed to me.
157. I enjoy applying God's promises to seemingly impossible situations.

158. I can identify elements of truth or of error when I hear or read the teachings of others.
159. Sometimes key church leaders talk to me about their needs and their problems.
160. I can lead a committee in making decisions.
161. I feel that, if needed, I would have many spiritual gifts that would equip me to minister in a first generation Christian congregation.
162. I do not mind speaking the truth even at the risk of confronting those in places of authority.
163. I enjoy going where non-Christians congregate in order to win them for Christ.
164. I feel very strongly that a Christian congregation should be unified.
165. I like to deduce biblical principles from my study and then share them with others.
166. Frequently my ministry consists of watching for unmet needs and then quietly meeting those needs.
167. People will take correction from me because they know I'm on their side.
168. Occasionally I sense that some appeals for money are not worthy appeals.
169. God enables me to develop plans that will assist others to fulfill a ministry of helping.
170. Sometimes I feel so compassionate for others that I fail to confront them with the truth when they need it.
171. Through prayer God sometimes helps me to impart physical healing to others.
172. The Holy Spirit sometimes works immediately to change situations when I pray in faith.
173. Sometimes in prayer I feel such an overwhelming burden to praise or to intercede that I cannot find words with which to express myself.
174. When I have heard tongues interpreted I knew that the one interpreting was not truly being led by the Holy

Spirit because God gave me the proper interpretation.

175. God uses me to bring clarity to others when they are uncertain about what to do.

176. Sometimes I have become aware of something that happened to another person that caused him to act as he did.

177. Through prayer I can tap into God's power on behalf of others.

178. I have detected an element of pride and self-glory in the ministries of some speakers that are highly acclaimed by many others.

179. I enjoy helping others so that they, in turn, can perform ministries that I can't do.

180. I can lead others in matters of planning and in deploying the abilities of the group.

181. I feel relaxed and confident even when I am standing alone for Christ in a hostile, non-Christian environment.

182. I enjoy applying biblical principles to the present day.

183. I think God has given me or wants to give me the gift of evangelism.

184. I am interested in the details of the lives of others so that I can help them grow as Christ's disciples.

185. I want to know the authoritative basis before I accept any statement as valid.

186. I enjoy serving others physically or materially in order to make their burdens lighter.

187. I seem to have the ability to call forth the best that is in others.

188. When I give to Christian ministries it is important to me that my decision to give be confirmed by my spouse or by other Christians that I respect.

189. Other Christians have called me a natural-born leader.

190. I can cheerfully spend time with those who need someone to listen to them.

191. I like to pray for those who are physically and

emotionally ill.

192. I have been God's instrument to effect supernatural changes in circumstances or in lives.
193. Praying in tongues helps me to be a better Christian and a better church member.
194. When I interpret tongues I usually do so with a view of how unbelievers can be edified or helped.
195. At times God gives me a wisdom beyond my natural abilities.
196. Often God has helped me focus in on a problem even though others were not aware that there was a problem.
197. I enjoy spending long periods of time in prayer in behalf of others.
198. I sense when teachers are prompted by the Holy Spirit, or by an evil spirit, or merely by their own human spirit.
199. I prefer to receive no public thanks for the little things I do to help others.
200. I can see the total picture easier than some others, and I can use my insights to give guidance.

List below your top three or four scores.

| Gift | Score |
|------|-------|
| _____ | _____ |
| _____ | _____ |
| _____ | _____ |
| _____ | _____ |

Some people tend to respond more conservatively than others. Therefore, no standard can be determined for qualifying one as having a particular spiritual gift. A total of fifty points is possible under each gift. Many Christians find that they will score 30 or 35 or above on two, three, or four spiritual gifts.

# The Key

A    Apostleship

B    Prophecy

C    Evangelism

D    Shepherding

E    Teaching

F    Serving

G    Exhortation

H    Giving

I    Giving Aid

J    Compassion

K    Healing

L    Working Miracles

M    Tongues

N    Interpretation of Tongues

O    Wisdom

P    Knowledge

Q    Faith

R    Discernment

S    Helps

T    Administration

# A Selected Bibliography for the Further Study of The Gifts of the Spirit

Dr. Kenneth Cain Kinghorn

I have listed below a number of books that I consider to contain the best treatment of spiritual gifts. These volumes are written from a variety of theological viewpoints, and some of them will provide more help than others. Consequently, I have indicated with an asterisk (*) the books that stand out as particularly helpful.

Bittlinger, Arnold. *Gifts and Graces.* Grand Rapids: Wm. B. Eerdmans Publishing Co., 1967.

*Bridge, Donald and David Pyphers. *Spiritual Gifts and the Church.* Downers Grove: Inter-Varsity Press, 1973.

Criswell, W.A. *The Baptism, Filling and Gifts of the Holy Spirit.* Grand Rapids: Zondervan Publishing Co., 1973.

*Flynn, Leslie B. *Nineteen Gifts of the Spirit.* Wheaton: Victor Books, 1974.

*Gangel, Kenneth O. *You and Your Spiritual Gifts.* Chicago: Moody Press, 1975.

Gee, Donald. *Concerning Spiritual Gifts.* Springfield, MO: Gospel Publishing House, 1928.

Grossman, Siegfried. *Charisma, the Gifts of the Spirit.* Wheaton: Key Publishers, Inc., 1971.

—————————. *There are Other Gifts than Tongues.* Wheaton: Tyndale House Publishers, 1971.

*Kinghorn, Kenneth Cain. *Gifts of the Spirit.* Nashville: Abingdon Press, 1976.

Koch, Kurt. *Charismatic Gifts.* Quebec, Canada: The Association for Christian Evangelism, 1975.

MacGorman, Jack W. *The Gifts of the Spirit.* Nashville: Broadman Press, 1974.

*McRae, William J. *The Dynamics of Spiritual Gifts.* Grand Rapids: Zondervan Publishing Co., 1976.

Murphy, Edward F. *Spiritual Gifts and the Great Commission.* South Pasadena: Mandate Press, 1975.

O'Connor, Elizabeth. *Eighth Day of Creation.* Waco, TX: Word Books, 1971.

Purkiser, W.T. *The Gifts of the Spirit.* Kansas City: Beacon Hill Press, 1975.

Steadman, Ray. *Body Life.* Glendale: Regal Books, 1972.

*Yohn, Rick. *Discover Your Spiritual Gift.* Wheaton: Tyndale House Publishers, 1974.

*Wagner, C. Peter. *Your Spiritual Gifts Can Help Your Church Grow.* Glendale: Regal Books, 1979.